WORKBOOK

for use with

Staying One

How to Avoid a Make-Believe Marriage

Clinton W. McLemore

CASCADE *Books* · Eugene, Oregon

STAYING ONE
How to Avoid a Make-Believe Marriage: Workbook

Cascade Books
An Imprint of Wipf and Stock Publishers
199 W. 8th Ave., Suite 3
Eugene, OR 97401

www.wipfandstock.com

PAPERBACK ISBN: 978-1-4982-9548-2
EBOOK ISBN: 978-1-4982-9549-9

Cataloguing-in-Publication data:

Names: McLemore, Clinton W. | McLemore, Anna M.

Title: Staying one : how to avoid a make-believe marriage : workbook/ Clinton W. McLemore with Anna M. McLemore.

Description: Eugene, OR: Cascade Books, 2017

Identifiers: ISBN 978-1-4982-9548-2 (paperback) | ISBN 978-1-4982-9549-9 (ebook)

Subjects: LCSH: Marriage—Religious aspects—Christianity. | Married people—Psychology. | Married people—Conduct of life.

Classification: BV835 M253 2017 (print) | BV835 (ebook)

Manufactured in the U.S.A.   FEBRUARY 15, 2017

Introduction

IN *STAYING ONE,* I highlight the difference between *knowing how* and *knowing that*. In attempting to learn to swim, you might study all about buoyancy, hydrodynamic efficiency, and how specific movements of the human body help counter gravitational pull. But none of this, by itself, would get you any closer to learning to keep yourself afloat. You could spend a lifetime becoming the world's greatest expert on the physics of swimming, and you might still not know how.

When I took a sailing course years ago, I spent hours in a classroom where the instructor made sure we understood the fundamentals of tacking and jibing. But he knew that this was only preparation and that none of us would learn how to sail without hands-on practice. So, out onto the water we went.

View this workbook as a way to practice marital sailing. It will provide you with opportunities for putting into practice what you learn in the book. The twenty exercises it contains have been carefully crafted to be non-threatening and are unlikely to paint either you or your spouse into a corner.

To get everything you can from these exercises, engage with them *actively*. Don't just read through them. This means that you'll have to *write* out your answers and also record what your spouse says. I cannot overemphasize the importance of this. People find it far easier to remember what they note down. They are also more likely to follow through with written commitments. At the end of this booklet, you will find several pages on which you can take notes from *Staying One*, and if you are using it in conjunction with a workshop, also from what the workshop leader says.

Returning to the metaphor of sailing, my hope is that *Staying One* will help you navigate the waters of your marriage and help you chart a course toward the marriage your heavenly Father intends for you. As you make your way through the exercises, I pray that doing them will bless both you and your spouse.

Exercise #1: YOUR DE-ESCALATING STRATEGIES AND TACTICS

INSTRUCTIONS: Identify and write down strategies or tactics you have used at least once to slow down or stop negative escalation. Which ones do you believe it would be good to use more frequently?

_____

_____

_____

_____

_____

_____

_____

_____

_____

Exercise #2: YOUR SPOUSE'S DE-ESCALATING STRATEGIES AND TACTICS

INSTRUCTIONS: Identify and write down the de-escalating strategies or tactics your spouse has used. Are there any you'd like to adopt?

_____

_____

_____

_____

_____

_____

_____

_____

_____

_____

Exercise #3: WHAT YOU MOST APPRECIATE

INSTRUCTIONS: Write down what you most appreciate about your spouse. Complete this sentence: *"What I appreciate about you is . . ."*

_____

_____

_____

_____

_____

_____

_____

_____

_____

Exercise #4: EXPRESSING APPRECIATION

INSTRUCTIONS: Speak the words that you wrote for Exercise #3. And, if your spouse did Exercise #3, write down, here, what he or she tells you.

_____

_____

_____

_____

_____

_____

_____

_____

Exercise #5: MODES OF LOVE YOU BELIEVE YOU MOST USE

Here are ten modes of expressing love:

1. Providing for Your Spouse

2. Assisting Your Spouse

3. Sharing Space and Time

4. Conveying Empathy

5. Verbalizing Affection

6. Sexual Expression

7. Non-sexual Touch

8. Siding With and Supporting

9. Cherishing and Respecting

10. Helping Your Spouse Reach Full Potential

INSTRUCTIONS: Write down, in order, which modes you _believe_ you use most often to express love to your spouse. Of the ten, which ones do you tend to rely on? First, list the mode you use most frequently. Then, write down the one you believe you use second most frequently. And, so on.

1. _____

_____

2. _____

_____

3. _____

_____

4. _____

_____

5. _____

_____

6. _____

_____

7. _____

_____

8. _____

_____

9. _____

_____

10. _____

_____

Exercise #6: MODES OF LOVE YOU BELIEVE YOUR SPOUSE DESIRES

INSTRUCTIONS: List the modes of love you believe your spouse most wants from you. Again, write them down in order, from highest to lowest in importance. Try to list every one that you see as having any importance in your marriage.

1. _____

_____

2. _____

_____

3. _____

_____

4. _____

_____

5. _____

_____

6. _____

_____

7. _____

_____

8. _____

_____

9. _____

_____

10. _____

_____

Exercise #7: MODES OF LOVE YOU MOST DESIRE

INSTRUCTIONS: Write out the modes of love you would like even more of. Once again, list them in order of importance.

1. _____

_____

2. _____

_____

3. _____

_____

4. _____

_____

5. _____

_____

6. _____

_____

7. _____

_____

8. _____

_____

9. _____

_____

10. _____

_____

Exercise #8: MODES OF LOVE YOUR SPOUSE
ACTUALLY DESIRES

INSTRUCTIONS: Ask your spouse and *write down* what he or she would like even more of (what he or she wrote for Exercise #7). Then, reverse roles.

1. _____

_____

2. _____

_____

3. _____

_____

4. _____

_____

5. _____

_____

Exercise #9: WHAT YOU DO VERSUS WHAT
YOUR SPOUSE WANTS

INSTRUCTIONS: Compare what you've written as the modes of love you believe you most use (Exercise #5) with the ones your spouse would like more of (Exercise #8). *Write down* whatever differences you notice.

_____

_____

_____

_____

_____

_____

_____

_____

_____

Exercise #10: CHECKING ON THE ACCURACY
OF YOUR ASSUMPTIONS

INSTRUCTIONS: Compare what your spouse told you about the modes of love he or she would like more of (Exercise #8) with what you _assumed_ was most important to your spouse (Exercise #6). _Write down_ your observations.

_____

_____

_____

_____

_____

_____

_____

_____

Exercise #11: TOWARD MORE CONSTRUCTIVE
CONVERSATIONS

INSTRUCTIONS: Look over the list of fourteen principles below and circle the ones you most need to follow. You do not have to share this information with your spouse. Whether or not you do is up to you.

1. Stick to the issue
2. Avoid the use of *always* and *never.*
3. Take breaks when you need them.
4. Don't hurl psychiatric labels.
5. Keep your arguments private.
6. Refrain from threats of divorce.
7. Stay away from moralistic slurs, sexual insults, or sarcastic slights.
8. Keep it verbal.
9. Allow your spouse to save face.
10. Focus on slow feelings.
11. Put an end to mind reading.
12. Use mirroring.
13. Be wary of *but.*
14. Use *I* statements.

Exercise #12: WHAT GETS NEGOTIATED IN YOUR MARRIAGE

INSTRUCTIONS: Write down some of the more important things that get negotiated in your marriage. What, precisely, has to be decided? Then, specify *how often* you negotiate these issues.

_____

_____

_____

_____

_____

_____

_____

_____

_____

_____

_____

_____

Exercise #13: NEGOTIATIONS THAT MIGHT HAVE GONE BETTER

INSTRUCTIONS: Review what you wrote for Exercise #12. Identify any negotiations that faltered or failed, even if only temporarily and you were later able to come to a resolution. Then, write down what *you* might have done differently.

_____

_____

_____

_____

_____

_____

_____

_____

_____

_____

_____

Exercise #14: COMMON AREAS OF TENSION IN MARRIAGES

INSTRUCTIONS: What do you believe married couples most often argue about?

_____

_____

_____

_____

_____

_____

_____

_____

_____

_____

Exercise #15: AREAS OF TENSION IN YOUR MARRIAGE

INSTRUCTIONS: What do the two of you continually have the most conflict over?

_____

_____

_____

_____

_____

_____

_____

_____

_____

_____

Exercise #16: WHAT WOULD YOU LIKE EVEN MORE OF FROM YOUR SPOUSE?

INSTRUCTIONS: Write down what you would like even more of from your spouse.

_____

_____

_____

_____

_____

_____

_____

_____

_____

_____

Exercise #17: LOVING AND SUPPORTING YOUR SPOUSE

INSTRUCTIONS: Ask your spouse how you might be able to provide more love and support, and write down what he or she tells you: How can I support you?

_____

_____

_____

_____

_____

_____

_____

_____

Exercise #18: DRAFTING YOUR MARITAL COMPACT

INSTRUCTIONS: Draft your marital compact, using this form: "I (husband's name) commit to doing the following" (after which comes a list of specific behaviors) and "I (wife's name) commit to doing the following" (after which comes another list of concrete behaviors).

I (Husband) commit to doing the following:

_____

_____

_____

_____

_____

_____

_____

_____

I (Wife) commit to doing the following:

_____
_____
_____
_____
_____
_____
_____
_____
_____
_____
_____
_____
_____

Exercise #19: MAKING THE COMMITMENT

INSTRUCTIONS: Sign your compact and say to your spouse, "In the name of the Father, the Son, and the Holy Spirit, I will endeavor to honor this agreement to the best of my ability."

_____   _____
Husband   **Wife**

_____
Date

Exercise #20: WRITING A LETTER

INSTRUCTIONS: Write a letter to your husband or wife, in which you express affection and appreciation. Photocopy it and then mail the copy to him or her when you get home.

_____

_____

_____

_____

_____

_____

_____

_____

_____

_____

_____

_____

_____

_____

_____

_____

_____

_____

_____

_____

_____

_____

Notes from the Workshop

_____

_____

_____

_____

_____

_____

_____

_____

_____

_____

_____

_____

_____

_____

_____

_____

_____

_____

_____

_____

_____

_____

_____

_____

_____

_____

_____

_____

Notes from the Workshop

Notes from the Workshop

Notes from the Workshop

Notes from the Workshop

Notes from the Workshop

www.ingramcontent.com/pod-product-compliance
Lightning Source LLC
Chambersburg PA
CBHW081244020426
42331CB00013B/3289